"IT'S NEVER TOO LATE
TO HAVE A HAPPY CHILDHOOD"

You were once a
wondrous, joyous,
creative, curious, innocent
child.

That special inner child
remains with you today.

Honor, celebrate, and
acknowledge that child.

"IT'S NEVER TOO LATE TO HAVE A HAPPY CHILDHOOD"

Inspirations for Adult Children

CLAUDIA BLACK

Paintings by Laurie Zagon

Ballantine Books · New York

Library of Congress Catalog Card Number: 89-90825

ISBN: 0-345-36279-9

Cover design by James R. Harris
Cover painting by Laurie Zagon: Light of Ecstasy, 1988,
oil on canvas, 48″ x 24″
Text design by Alexander J. Klapwald

Manufactured in the United States of America

First Edition: October 1989
10 9 8 7 6 5 4 3 2 1

To my brother, Doug, who brought love, light, and color into my life.

—Claudia

Acknowledgments

I would like to acknowledge Laurie Zagon, whose works of art so clearly speak to the energy, color, and light in each and every one of us. Laurie's spirit is reflected not only in her paintings—it is also illuminated in her being. I am honored to have had an opportunity for such a special collaboration.

Laurie and I would both like to acknowledge our editor, Cheryl Woodruff. Thank you Cheryl for the original conception of *"It's Never Too Late to Have a Happy Childhood."* Thank you for bringing us together.

Introduction

While my previous books have primarily addressed Adult Children of Alcoholics, *"It's Never Too Late to Have a Happy Childhood"* is meant for anyone who for any reason is learning for the first time to "parent" themselves in a manner that may never have been available to them as children. It is a book that reminds us that no matter how much we approach our lives from an adult frame of mind, within us remains an "inner child"—the part of us that doesn't disappear just because we have grown in height and weight.

The concept of the Adult Child was originally developed to help validate and support individuals who were once raised in a chemically dependent or otherwise dysfunctional family system and who now, as adults, find their lives often filled with profound psychological, emotional, and even physical consequences rooted in their childhood experiences. Today, the term Adult Child has been expanded to apply to anyone who has experienced "loss on a chronic basis" during their childhood years—and it is a concept that is relevant to anyone committed to reclaiming their full humanity.

Recovery for Adult Children lies in their taking responsibility to go back and explore the past of their childhood in order to reclaim their "inner child." This book is a special tribute to the "inner child"—that wondrous little being inside each and every one of us that lets us know that it's never too late to begin the experience of self-discovery.

The thirty-four inspirational messages in this book are designed to replace the hurtful messages of our childhood. It is by reframing these hurtful messages that we can begin to live in a way that allows us to reconnect with our transcendant human spirit. Reclaiming the Self lost in childhood doesn't have to be overwhelming and immobilizing. Recovery can also be fun and exciting—an unexpected gift that can inspire one's sense of inner peace and serenity.

It has been an honor to bring messages that I hope you will find inspiring together with the paintings of artist Laurie Zagon. Laurie's work reflects my belief that every person's life is a rich tapestry of color, energy, and light. Every person's life story is distinctively colorful. We often lose this sense of our own inner richness because we become disconnected from our inner child. The vibrancy of color in Laurie's work truly reflects the process of recovery—an ongoing process of growth and movement that is sometimes astonishingly subtle and at other times intense and dramatic.

Laurie's vision of the triumphant human spirit is a perspective that I certainly share. As Laurie says, "I believe that the inner light within all of us is sometimes dimmed because of certain painful experiences, but what I attempt to do in my art is to show that even our pain can be transformed by letting in even the smallest ray of light—one moment of penetrating consciousness can open the window to the soul and allow our inner greatness and joy to surface once more."

It is our hope that "*It's Never Too Late to Have a Happy Childhood*" will be an ongoing gift you give to yourself at those moments when life most threatens your serenity. And that it will remind you to take time out in your day to re-center yourself.

May these messages help you tap into your inner strength and wisdom at the times when you are feeling most vulnerable. May they provide ongoing validation for what you are discovering on the path of your own self-healing. May "*It's Never Too Late to Have a Happy Childhood*" remind you that you are a kaleidoscope of colors, constantly shifting and changing.

In love,
CLAUDIA BLACK
OCTOBER 1989

"IT'S NEVER TOO LATE
TO HAVE A HAPPY CHILDHOOD"

You are very special.

You may never have had the opportunity to believe in your specialness.

You may believe in it today.

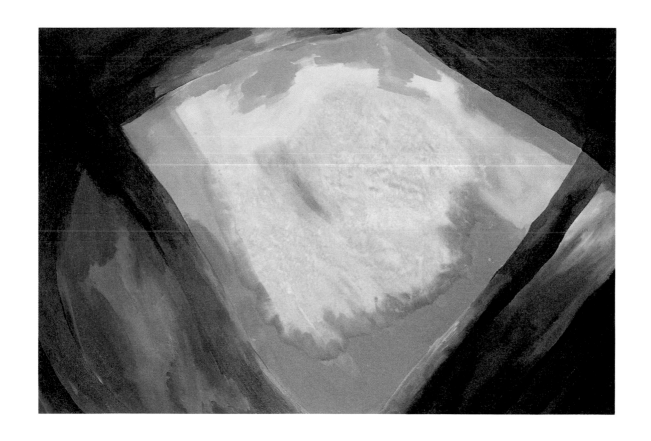

You deserve to no longer live your life in fear.

Recovery is not a solitary journey.

Even if you could do it alone you don't deserve to do it alone.

To free yourself from the past, you must break the
rules of silence and compliance.

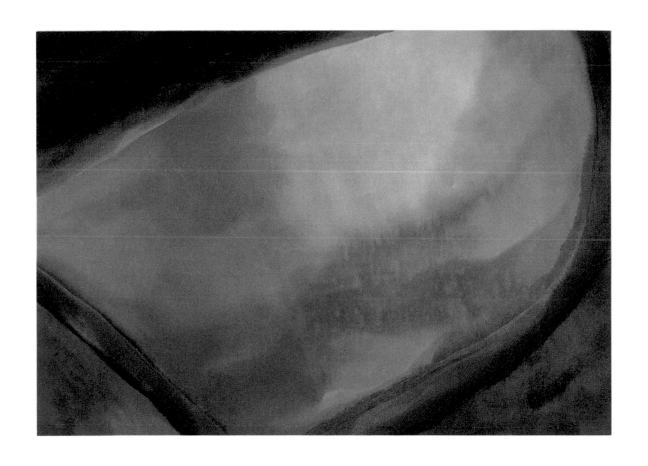

No one can go forward without finishing with the past.

It is not the mountain that gets moved that makes a difference.

It is the little steps taken, one at a time.

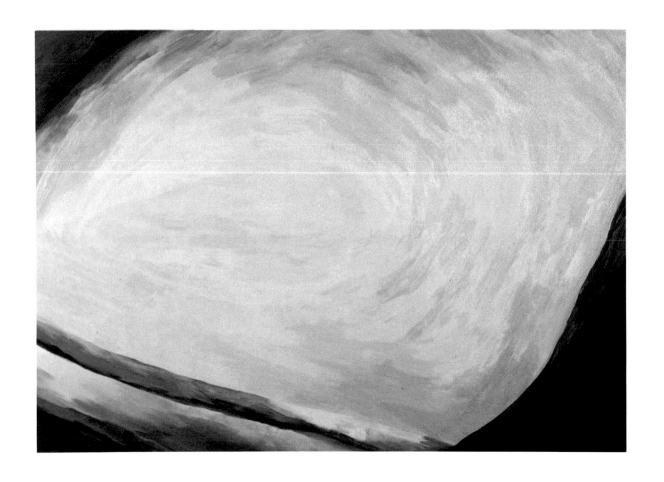

There is no perfect recovery.

Recovery is a process not an event.

One needs to walk through the pain,
    not over it,
    not around it.

You never again have to walk through it alone.

Where there is loss there are tears.

Tears are the elixir of recovery.

Feelings are from your heart and what your heart wants to tell you.

Feelings are to be listened to—they are cues and signals that indicate where you are and what you need.

You may have many feelings at the same time. They may seem to contradict each other.

This does not mean you are going crazy.

It means you are having many feelings at the same time.

The fears of what will happen if you express your feelings are often based in your childhood.

Today you can respond with the vulnerability of your child but with the strength of your adult.

Listen to your inner child not with criticism but with openness.

Anger does not have to mean a lessening of love. It does not have to mean hate.

Anger means to be angry.

It need not have an additional meaning.

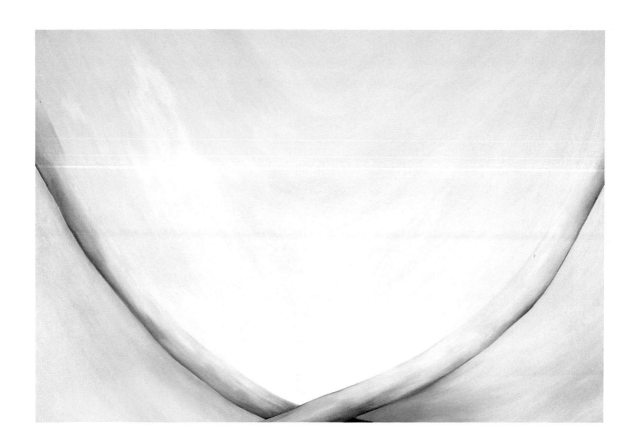

Love the child for all she had to defend against.

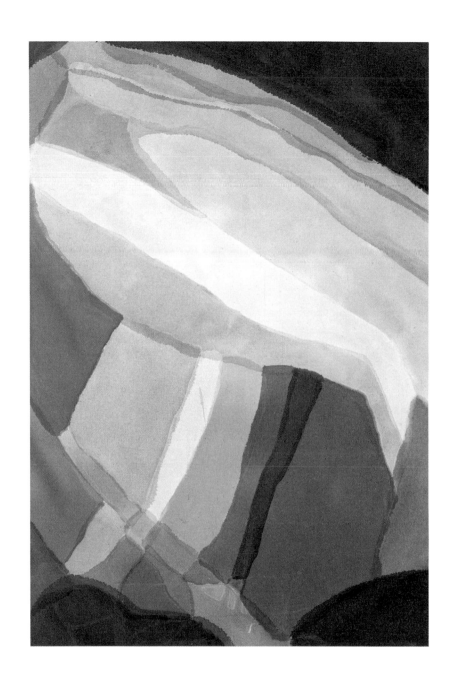

The fear of abandonment can be put behind you.

There are people who care.

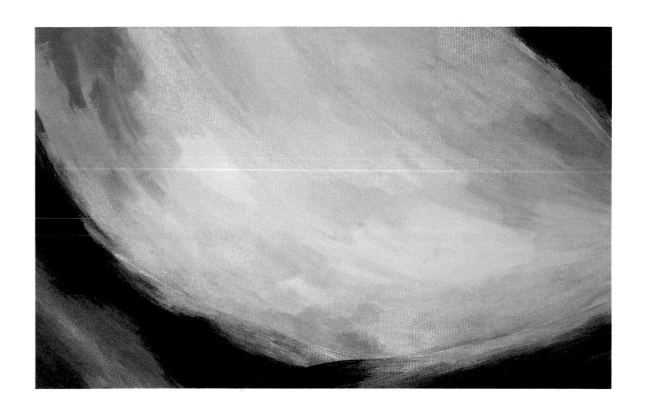

Faith is the result of learning to trust and to let go.

In faith one finds the strength to survive times of great fear and sadness.

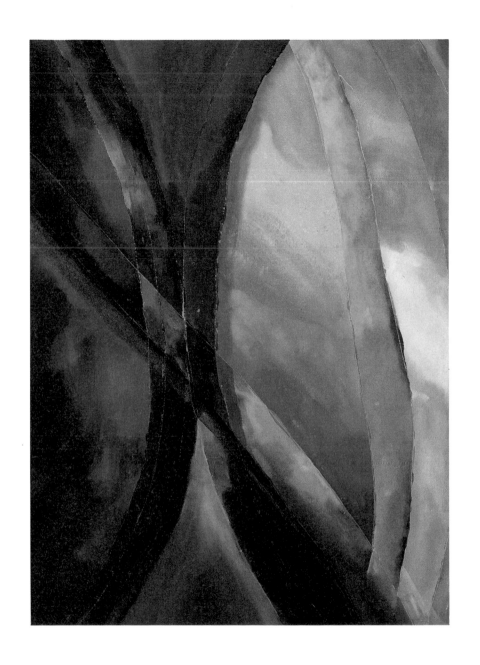

*When you have faith you give up the need to
control.*

Faith and control cannot peacefully co-exist.

Forgiving is not forgetting.

It is remembering and letting go.

Trust in yourself.

Your perceptions are often far more accurate than you are willing to believe.

Your needs are important.

Believing you deserve to have your needs met is as crucial as being able to identify your needs.

You have the right to say "no."

Saying no can be the ultimate self-care.

No and yes are a part of the same continuum. No and yes are choices.

Being less than perfect makes you human.

The greater your inner strength, and your ability to trust in yourself, the more willing you are to take risks.

Mistakes are a sign of growing.

Remember, be gentle with yourself.

Surround yourself with people who respect and treat you well.

May you come to cherish
both your masculine and
feminine strengths.

It is safe to take time to play today.

Play fuels your creativity, tickles your inner child,
and nurtures your soul.

Recovery is accepting yourself for who you are—no longer waiting for others to define you or to approve of you.

Success is not relative to others.

It is a feeling of love and accomplishment for yourself.

Does the pain ever go away?

Yes.

You are good enough!

You are good enough!

You are good enough!

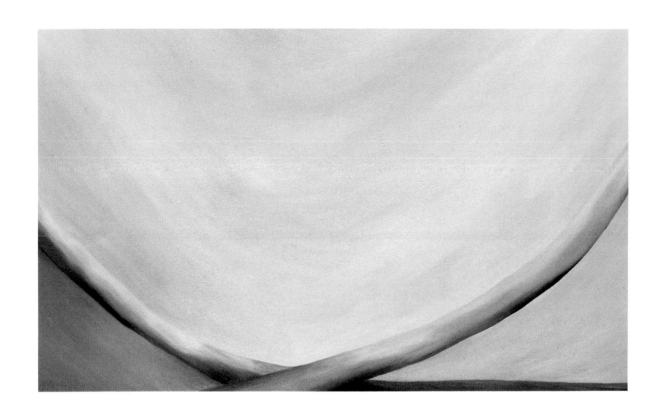

May the child in your heart remain forever free.

Paintings by Laurie Zagon

frontispiece *Window to Destiny*, 1988, oil on canvas, 72" X 36"

1. *White Light Sunday*, 1985, oil on canvas, 47" X 68"
2. *Having Seen Bonnard*, 1984, acrylic on canvas, 46" X 68"
3. *JCL*, 1980, acrylic on canvas, 40" X 68"
4. *Manhattan Sun Dance*, 1984, acrylic on canvas, 46" X 68"
5. *Craywinckel*, 1983, acrylic on canvas, 40" x 30"
6. *Sunset on Fire Island*, 1988, oil on canvas, 22½" X 59"
7. *Centrifical Rush*, 1984, acrylic on canvas, 47" X 66"
8. *Thoughts of 22nd Street*, 1983, acrylic on canvas, 47" X 29½"
9. *Soaring in Jamaica*, 1987, oil on canvas, 40" X 68"
10. *From the 4th Center*, 1987, oil on canvas, 40" X 68"
11. *Inside Ecstasy*, 1985, acrylic on canvas, 47" X 68"
12. *Open Light*, 1985, oil on canvas, 47" X 68"
13. *Pure Spirits*, 1985, oil on canvas, 30" X 48"
14. *Land and Sea*, 1988, oil on canvas, 30" X 80"
15. *Venice*, 1986, oil on canvas, 47" X 68"
16. *DD and the BBC*, 1980, acrylic on canvas, 24" X 36"
17. *Gold Edge with Remnants of Pink Flamingos*, 1985, acrylic on canvas, 30" X 48"
18. *Warm Changes*, 1984, acrylic on canvas, 67" X 48½"
19. *Waiting for the Sea*, 1985, acrylic on canvas, 17" X 28½"
20. *Identity*, 1985, acrylic on canvas, 30" X 48"
21. *Clearwater*, 1984, acrylic on canvas, 48" X 96"
22. *Advancing into Light*, 1986, oil on canvas, 80" X 30"
23. *Insight of LS*, 1987, oil on canvas, 47" X 68"
24. *Chip's Painting*, 1987, oil on canvas, 30" X 80"
25. *Sit Down for Twenty*, 1980, acrylic on canvas, 47" X 68"
26. *Riding Steps*, 1981, acrylic on canvas, 40" X 68"
27. *Homage to Turner*, 1988, oil on canvas, 24" X 18"
28. *Atlantean Garden*, 1987, oil on canvas, 66" X 92"
29. *Almunecar*, 1980, acrylic on canvas, 38" X 68"
30. *Truth and Love*, 1987, oil on canvas, 48" X 30"
31. *Jess*, 1986, oil on canvas, 47" X 68"
32. *Light of Ecstasy*, 1988, oil on canvas, 48" X 24"
33. *Divine Light*, 1985, oil on canvas, 49" X 68"

About the Author

Claudia Black is an acknowledged pioneer in the field of family therapy, known for her unique ability to illuminate and explain the special problems faced by those raised in dysfunctional families.

Her early works, *My Dad Loves Me, My Dad Has a Disease, Repeat After Me,* and the million-copy bestseller *"It Will Never Happen to Me,"* are recognized as classics in the recovery field for Adult Children of Alcoholics. A skilled therapist and an exceptional teacher, Dr. Black has educated thousands worldwide through her lectures and films.

Dr. Black is a founding board member of The National Association for Children of Alcoholics, sits on the board of TARGET, the National Federation of State High School Associations, and is the recipient of many National awards in the addiction field.

Claudia lives in Laguna Beach, California, where she has discovered much of the beauty and peace found in this book.

About the Artist

Artist Laurie Zagon has been a professor of color and light theory for over fourteen years. She is a lecturer and consultant, and co-founder of The Color Collective Council of America—a consortium of color experts dedicated to the advancement of color theory and color psychology. Her works have been exhibited throughout the world and are featured in prominent private collections such as those of Prudential Insurance and The Manufacturers Hanover Trust Company. Ms. Zagon's work is profiled in *New York Review of the Arts.*

Ms. Zagon resides in New York City.